THE RUINED ELEGANCE

PRINCETON SERIES OF CONTEMPORARY POETS

Susan Stewart, *series editor*

For other titles in the Princeton Series of Contemporary Poets see page 63

THE RUINED ELEGANCE

Poems

Fiona Sze-Lorrain

PRINCETON UNIVERSITY PRESS
Princeton & Oxford

ISBN 978-0-691-16750-3

ISBN (pbk.) 978-0-691-16769-5

Library of Congress Control Number: 2014959230

British Library Cataloging-in-Publication Data is available

This book has been composed in Adobe Garamond and Scala Sans

Printed on acid-free paper. ∞

Printed in the United States of America

10 9 8 7 6 5 4 3 2 1

Contents

Be the bliss of my trembling
like a tree's leaves:
give a name, give a beautiful name
a pillow to this disintegration.
    —JÁNOS PILINSZKY

(I)

WRONG EPIC

GIVEN SILENCE

saliva pressed on wax paper

in a china cup, the cracks let me think

a black sorrowful elk

assassinated in its postpartum shock

luck wasted at a state banquet

backward and forward the story is doctored

closer to laughter—the smell

of paulownia

a nun stood beside me, *which stone in what box*

TOWERING

Are you interested in stealing
instincts? Or in explaining
secrets of a world
that rules with age and equidistance?

Layer by layer, wind
seeks a message,
a voice for Fate. The sun,
its seas,
even birds in passing,
dictate science at the bidding of will.
An existence
unaffected by seasons.

So much about an unfathomable life.
A round universe with plans for tomorrow,
never its final word.

I can't speak for accidents elsewhere,
only forms, lines—
thoughts stretching to dialogue
on charts or water.
Believe me,
answers are small

even if one day you travel
in light years,
even when light becomes endless
as a star dies, another
emerges, in astonishment
and for no reason.

I WAIT FOR THE RUINED ELEGANCE

Plum blossoms comb the southern mountain. Maybe
    winter,

maybe spring. What can the difference

give a bystander? If

only swallows mend the wind, another way to choose—
tree to tree, grievance
                by grievance. I watch

the sun turn from a sphere to a palace. Burning,

but not disastrous. Soon, or
    now, my gaze

will break. I want to honor

the invisible. I'll use the fog to see white peaches.

BACK FROM THE AEGEAN SEA

Oracles die in this folktale. Thinking that I must harness the past, I erase temples and scriptoria, civilizations buried in Persian tombs. Disrobed of their worth, revived in museums. Twice I paid to stand close to the sacred. I stood on the rim of an emptiness, losing deities no matter how I asked. In an era not mine I couldn't trust a guide. This was the atmosphere I had been after in different libraries and editions. A compulsion to hold the weight of myths. How about histories, legacies that emperors tailored to their will. If gods were masters of their fates, are we the guests of our inner lives. Speaking of heroes who submit to egos. I am attracted to the tragic ones. To question the options of elegy, I've probably chosen the wrong epic.

IN THE THICK OF IT

> To turn magnified trouser legs / Into savoury tripe.
> —GU CHENG (1956–1993), "WHO'D HAVE THOUGHT?"

Gu Cheng's hat performed an exorcism.

Stovepipe, a leg

cut from old jeans, it
helped him feel kingly—relieved
of why and megalomania.

Maybe he wore it
to imagine
the year two thousand. Or his wife's
new pregnancy.

Turning his head, a utopia.

The hat is as real as a space reserved

for a long, terrible sleep.

Like a pagoda on the level plain, it
looked out,
farther—
over a world flooded with lights.

Of course,

I don't know who Gu Cheng was.

I think of his sketches, erasures,
what is found

in his verses,
lost in translation, sleepwalking

in a fight
between image and its less tender life.

IONIAN SUPPER

Let's not discuss politics. Exits made in haste, an extra glass of wine. A young lad taunts a duchess with a line from Ibsen. Talks her home with a harp in mind. *Praise the food*, a mother nods to her child. Night turns Babylonian, I can't swear for what isn't pleasant. Will you control the leftovers. Men speak of their horses where kindness should have been. Let us think of the guests as drunken stars. They lie to one another because they want to shine. Self-portraits—*I have, I want.* Story after story in spite of time. Details morph into affairs darker than adventures. How far can wisdom go. Can you listen without a narrative sense of self. I imagine my husband's conspicuous ear, governed by no indifference, no secret.

PARTITA, BUT NOTHING TO DO WITH BACH

In an herbarium-now-café, winter drops its guard.
      Write is to stay at the crime scene from the start.

I detect traitors and sleep dangerously. Stallions
      on this vase, a prophecy to end. Touch their

manes—malleable, furring like a voice, a long-
      ago maiden who disperses into ether, ash-

held rivers. In ghost tales, forests are empires.
      I read Chinese when it is simplified. See

how its culture rips honor for prizes. Now
      and a century. Emperors and prayers. In this

fable, the crane stays injured. Swans twist
      their necks, but won't cry. Order reversed

after redemption. Here, an earthquake,
      the days, a slight fever. Plenty of others

sensitive to this poison. O raw island,
      do you suffer? *Morta la bestia, morto il veleno.*

Over geraniums and wild oranges, moths
      war for elegance like philosophers. Close

to light, picked by the hour. Upturned
      dunes, the moon—I climb its ladder. Why

these missing steps if troubadours
　　　sing them? Glad to resist the hardened

slur, my lute settles for a one-note aura.
　　　Volti subito—down the middle eight, for

better or worse. Do I want to curse when
　　　the thought is lopsided? Healing comes

slow, the wreckage perennial. Heat let go,
　　　it takes years to get silence right. I can't

write small. To stop. To sin. Not to linger.
　　　The music, a clarity that fails. That distance,

such a ritual. Let me breathe, in sleep I see
　　　coins and flashes. Like a pirate or a hawk,

plunder a fair wind. Rain liable to boreal
　　　summer, stones feel rounder. Jeweled

scent, our hollow earth, a plumy descent
　　　of the hunter's footsteps. A shadow reaches

him, after a comet tail. *Tell me straight,*
　　　it whispers, *about happiness with nothing*

outside. Still awake, I wait for Goya.
　　　In his world, lamps melt in terror. Pain

needs a mood, a style to reign. I see
　　　the painting inside my wound. Growing

up as trees turn into hospitals. My heart
　　　migrates from the air and the sea. Of

absence, of this alertness. To walk to what
    seems bright with the sun behind. I skip

dense sections—the grave and a macabre
    dance around a bonfire. To backtrack

from each scene, hear my derangements.
    Self-inflicted, but exposed for a reason. How

to cure? It's a routine. To dress well,
    to leave front seats free. To hold lyrics

hostage in each mouth. Szymanowski.
    Borodin. The touch is what's free to speak.

FEW DAYS BEFORE CHRISTMAS

Kim Jong-il was dead when I woke up and surfed
the net before my husband repeated
his curse that pigeons defecating on the balcony

should be cooked to no one's sorrow, even
if mourning was authentic and
wet butterflies stopped their wings to muse over strange flowers
I saw as hysteria.

(II)

IN A GODLESS TIME

BEGINNING

Between invocation and action, one must not let spirit
surrender. Speak properly, if they ask. Repeat for comfort,
there is a body outside a body. In this village, someone chants
a mantra, reads into the past without sacrifice. On horseback,
follow its time. Observe the feather, a revolution in the draft.
A dance, a struggle in each direction. As slow as possible. Year
by year, the altar burns. Altar burnt, they shut their blinds.

SPRING MASSACRE

Soldiers raped our cousin, over

and over.
No, these soldiers were in

fact students. They spoke English in
secret, dreamt

of sausages
and blond mistresses. Last

winter, in our courtyard, some helped
us plant

sunflowers—they grew

larger than our faces.

MAUSOLEUM

Father unearthed terracotta warriors
before his eyes turned half-blind on the same
day Red Guards scalped his sister's arms
bundled up with trash bags in a closet
no one found her until the edge of light
children were scavenging for walking sticks and rice
they found a broken vase and a stubborn
plant they said her eyes stuck out
like orange buns that bite they said his hair
turned white overnight

BACKSTAGE

News of Nixon's state visit spread from one labor
camp to the other. By force,

they nourished her with sautéed duck meat, crab
dumplings, ginseng, and longan.

She stopped plowing the acres with her capitalist
hands. Pulled out the zither

from its tomb under her bed, swaddled with
a drugged serpent, stitched

with dingy scarves. She plucked each string,
rehearsed her fear. Notes

took flight. The color of tears. Short tragedies,
part of a tunnel. Thrilled

to honor the first to laugh. Spirits in a fray,
twisted by ashflecks. Her lips

were parched. The strings stayed taut. None
broke. Her fingernails did.

DAY SEVEN

Early August.

Father's turn after they freed me
from prison. No more arresting figure of absence

than our tree—smoke

for face, dashes for arms, gone with bones
and vanity before the gate.

House, most of all. Half our clothes
burnt, most antiques

disappeared,
torn books and maps don't need forgiveness.

All things tentative, the house
wasn't. Come in,

come in—its breath
to the window, thuyas bend

for a riot, mountains into gray
propaganda,
        and my eyes—making do
with lines
quicker between mist, long since dry.

CENTER OF A JOURNEY

Doctors could not cure the hole in her heart. *Find witches to put out the fire in her eye*. Lamas predicted a sacrifice. In a canyon I carried her body when it died. The path wasn't hers, the view wasn't mine. We lived the weight of two and one. Orienting a life with no image or lie, she made decisions with seasons in her smile. To the sun, we emptied our pockets. To the walls, we slept with breasts shy. *Let's cup mustard seeds to your face and smell light*, she coaxed when rain couldn't take care of sad drama. It was difficult to lose sight. The burial or the shame—I couldn't say. A hole in her heart, an eye the nettle stung. Zeroing our past into a godless time.

AM I WHAT THE LAKE GAVE ME

Bent on music and heaven, the Prince of Chu named this place *a round wardrobe of tears*. The gazebo and the last trumpet call. Light is casual, but takes credit for the end. Only strangers need visiting privileges. Not all physicians make room for contradiction. One called my teacher sorceress before she drowned here. The rest, a matter not of reason. This is why our grief tastes like water. The children associate it with punishment. They have forgotten that water is an herb. Our sorceress will wake up at no distance. To linger or to pray. I tell myself I am safe. Five points and two maps, we are not from here, stopping to read signs from above. What a perfect question, a useless mirror.

MEDITATION

Labrang Monastery, 1955

Doors sealed. Night.
He resembles a tiger
waking up from a nightmare.
Winds change. The sky throws his roar.

He reaches a bridge
and tramples it down. Rushing north.
He throws the sky back,
thrusts his claws into iron bricks.

The bridge does not collapse,
its every bone shown.
Cicadas hiss. He starts to lick
a rectangular corpse.

Doors open. Morning hides its feet.
He resembles a scar
with no trace of blood,
the last shard of a massacre.

DUSTY CITADEL

Labrang Monastery, 2005

What hangs on tiers of prickled wires
to make a raging mind
picture nirvana between their holes,

Shangri-La in each square of air?
Mercy—on shadows that eat

cobblestones. This is where you wash
in the blood of fallen kings. Vertical
heart, a clock loses its face.
Jungles of hair lure the hungriest
tiger. No one arrives

after wrestling night. Whatever
spare limbs you stage fate on, carry
no message but the curse—
Pull it down.

(III)

THE BOOK, A SIMPLER GRAVE

TO WHOM IT MAY CONCERN

Accusation:

the imperial subject of reading
manners—

an Indian smears this page with fingers unwashed
in a prison lavatory.

Unzipping his pants, he imagines himself
as the Prime Minister
licking iced mocha balls in a man-made
savannah. Age isn't

a legal dispute:

his eyes savor a bottom with tattoos.
Wishing to hold them
in his palms—slippery molecules
swaying from side to side.

The warden comes, beats
him with a shoe. The Indian yells,
kicks his legs,
vomits yellow foam.

No muse protects him the way

Wilde set sail for Dieppe. He counts
down to the word
that makes this appeal light.

You'll be the judge. I, the indelible
blotch of ink,
swear to serve as your Bible,

the map of iron oaths,
its thundering silence,

each word an order,

the unbreakable chain of names and damns.

GRANTED ASYLUM

The buried book showed its teeth.

Under dust, but finished
with silence.

Pages moved their lips.

A faint odor. Ponds of saliva
the shape of loquat leaf.

The book was a gift.
Someone carved a date and "Dear X"
on its face.
Took short trips, fasted with it.

Its will healed

by absolution, for a nickel it regained
a body—the book

wanted a new country.

It held on
to its last chapter,

talisman against judgment.

AGAINST PROLOGUE

In the middle of the night, the heroine woke up realizing
she left the gods
in the dark
wet and naked, cloth over the eyes. Under her bed, two snakes
   glowered

holding back their thirst

[Stories are stolen even in sleep]

TO SURVIVE WHEN IT MUST

After its throat song,
        each clean quaver
        a curse,
the librarian believes
the tear of a page is a slit
of the book's tongue. Porous
and phantasmal, its blood
dries up
to quell terror. But
        the curse echoes
     deeper and beyond. The librarian
        knows the curse preserves a life.
In times of doubt, it'll fool
censors. It is mummified, it has eyes.
          She hears it day and night,
          in the silence of archives.

MIDNIGHT ALMANAC

Fugitive but wise, the line speaks to me. I can feel

its peristalsis.
A steppe, a map, an orientation.

The moon, a failed political party. Rain softens at no condition.

All the parallel windows, different emptiness.

The elf picked up a twig. Sat on a tomb slab. With juice from ferns he
cooled his fever, to nightwalkers he sang,

Take it easy now.

Discarded buses at a traveler's hour. A truck passed ahead. The
stoplight predicted father would return.

My city can heal water violin, water wings. If only you waited long
enough.

*A peach tree turns green after a thousand years. And the servants taste the
fruits quietly,* in the fable this is what happened before the snow. Here
is the truth: a girl considered violence under the tree, and the tree
couldn't turn her away.

Predator—One who reads aloud the ten grave precepts.
Mourn—Via finite waves.
Ajar—To return to the world where we first began, the breath and the
    body must be linear at each meal.
A Baroque guitar—The tavern is open for reservations.

Solitude—No, I burn diaries.

When the plot wore thin, Balzac deleted the moon from another town.

Torn by the lyric, the myth trailed like embers through the jade palace. A nymph in the clouds, light rippling behind. What road was left after the suspicion?

The sea, a sea with edges.

Are you not my caretaker. Ninety francs, informed by two letters.

What is buried in the earth grows out of the earth. I see in it a reminder. Of daily objects—buttons, toilet paper . . .

Samizdat.

The Petrarchan ideal.

A saucer, not a saucer. Quick memory in a coffee stain.

In my bed, spooning pear jam for my lover. Our silk duvet, neither form nor style. Let me give you all

before sleeping in your palm.

YIELD, PLEASE

Sleepless one, the stars contain their own triumphs.

Leave them behind. The sheer
glow of life.
                Tell the reader

why you're afraid to hide.

Ghosts do not dine at two tables at one
time. Let

alone us, princes who inherit

this static light.

[While this epitaph was found in a safe place]

ANNA AKHMATOVA, OR THE THOUGHTS
SHE DIDN'T WRITE

If Lev could telegraph his dreams from the Gulag
doors, my house had three
his letter began with *Mosquito, come* . . .
to keep the vigil, I'll give you mine

And fit sorrow into the mask of a requiem
house every stranger who leers with medial eyes
your ghost, Pushkin
sit with me in burial clothes
with a cigarette, mock at our toes flown

Before midgets tug at your skirt enthroned
think of how many times the moon can exist here, any of that
    allegiance
someone in the castle ransoms a native ghost

Wishing to still these lips with screaming gloves
for you and you to stab me without knives

AN UPRISING COMMITTED TO LONGHAND

> It is not in space that I must seek my human dignity,
> but in the ordering of my thought.
> —BLAISE PASCAL

In a corner where silence isn't obvious, I follow it until my gaze becomes a troupe of its kind. Elegant theories to tally scores and debts. Where punctuation marks stand sentry, a contemporary mob is walking on stilts. Transparency is distance unhinged. The scene now on the page, I wake to my five senses and an intuition. What begins as a weapon becomes a grain in my eye, bouncing here and here with no instruction. You can see weightlessness without feeling it. A figure defining the simplest. A grand *jeté* scissoring the space. These days I pursue a lightness in words. It is not space I stir, but a colorless peel off the written. Contained but free. Air that rises in a cup of soufflé. Just right there, never quite yet. A structure that works because it can open. Soluble sentences, portable terms. Cadences for landing birds and late apples.

GENEVIÈVE DE GAULLE-ANTHONIOZ TOOK MORE
THAN FIFTY YEARS BEFORE WRITING RAVENSBRÜCK
DOWN IN *LA TRAVERSÉE DE LA NUIT*

Trains derailed. She woke up, feeling history.
I'm posting letters behind a soldier's back.
Mind, a shrapnel shell for German figures of speech.
27 372—a five-digit indignity.
Non omnis moriar.
Scream. The Polish girl, Bacha?
Bone experiments. Without anesthesia.
They teased muscle fibers out with gloves and a naked eye.

She improvised psalms, built temples out of each, and abandoned
   them.
Stone, unalloyed.
No rehearsal between the murk and her, *would the dead take part in a
   photograph?*
She picked up an old match. [The past was here.]
Star, ghost, finger.

Floor and skin holing when they shouldn't be.
Mortar round one.
Mortar round two.
Clatter of a chain loosened the exorcism. Of spirits between hindgut
   and throat.
Someone, then no one.
The Communist said, *Twist the music in your head.*
At small hours, she culled Dante. Piecing up a suncatcher and names
   of the Saints.
Where the guards took a separate route, until the talk of treason.
Siren. Next in line.
Light hurt. The proof she took to stay alive.

CHOSEN BY THE NARRATOR

Q. whom we met for lunch at a Thai bistro,

writes poems on Hai Phong and the Viet Cong. Whoever lived
through war thinks her music isn't real.

Even the blue notes, python, and malaria. The sorceress

in this book pities Q. Grieves for her.
Who has chosen

ghosts for a career in Houston. One who isn't hers. The rest, not ours.

CANTABILE (MA STONATO)

after Giorgio Caproni

And they return, in times not ours.

Ancient longings and ancient
loves. Down the alley
of puppet faces,
uncommon flowers, walls
stay put when the sky can't balance.

The curses, the exorcisms,
devious mirrors, disfigured chapels,
footprints that prove
our existence ill-fated, after many
years and fake explanations.

They return. With the suicides, with children
stealing the last word
of unsung strangers.

(IV)

CAUGHT IN DEFIANCE

TRANSPARENT

At first I'd forgotten
its color.
An umbrella that couldn't open.
The aftermath of tears.
God's mask:
a mangosteen with worms.
To turn this ruined thought
into a poem,
I took out four words.

INK PAINTING FROM THE JOSEON DYNASTY

Open the scroll, a book of dawn.
Across a canyon's
chest, it slithers to a stop—

Cloud ship,
clear the horizon. It seals
like a scar, the wind
even. The next silence,
the next outcome
that fails.

A hermit waits.
A horse canters.
Mountain river thinks mountain
is river. Let ink. Let
air. A black
knife,
black tides of leaves
to slow a grave eastward.

If the moon struggles
in two stages,
unlock chakra with one eye
one finger. What comes to mind
won't stay on purpose.
Best to dwell
on a pinhole of light.
You are the seraphim,
a fortress in green-blue,
blinking and falling
into wakefulness.

WHAT'S LEFT OF A SIJO

A stillness, a ripple,
a prayerful
instant. I wait
because you
feign movement,
thin traces of a feckless
existence. An antelope,
a noble surprise.
Wind rises, eyes
follow this idle
stanza
to a pavilion,
a civilization at
the heart of the lake
where I know
ripples are still,
white ginger lilies
hesitate,
and you listen.

CHIAROSCURO, 2 A.M.

after Gao Xingjian

The disappeared returns
in obsidian. Are there two shadows
or am I near? Rooms apart,

the window begins here.
There is still time. Look for transparence
in an after-gray, shore

and space undone.
Where light is old and exits twice,
a liquid rebellion along the line.

Let me ride this hour into the dark—
weary birds return to my eyes,
leave me in the wake

of mixed metaphors, circular
travels. The outline
of a significant guest wanders

into the basement. What glows next
but a veil of no interest? This,
the last ghost caught in defiance.

BONNARD'S NAKED WIFE LEAVING THE BATHTUB

Marthe steps into a world her body knows
too well. Never too roundly
exposed for a smile.

Her face, no face, transcends
yellow. Like a lightbulb with an umbilical cord,
trying to straighten its life out.

Combing pubic hair with two fingers.

White lavender blue, orange green striped hues
seducing an eye without restraint.

You *must* look at her breasts.

Hold that thought, can you—while
relishing? Pluck me, she suggests

in quiet and style. Like a ripe plum,
she waits for a hand.
Toweling off a silver experience.

Here stands a moment in praise of mundane details,
quotidian rituals,
an improvisation without circumstances,
body stripped of alteration.

Like you, I wish for more narratives.
A plot that unravels a grand finale.

But we know imagination

trusts best in permanence—

Dawn held at a windowsill.
Drama shadowed where her feet are tipped off
by canvas and Pierre's calculation.

LA CHAMBRE D'ÉCOUTE

Magritte's green apple, luscious and imprisoned,
bigger
than a life
stalled forever,
caught me off guard with the sun up.

Unable to think of sequence and relief.

Perspective, a musical task.
A second way to the absence
and the real.

Next to a window,
decided
on balance, the color mutated
into grand failure.
Out of proportion, birthright at four
angles. That's the rule
about standstill. Why—I heard

the fruit,
its soft organs.

Coda or sequel, the potential din.
Tilting, slurring.
Levitating.
To obey the title like an amateur.
Disclaimer. But a mistress in search of her next lover.

THREE MOVES, CLOCKWISE

Kertész's fork resembles a fork
when the plate
that resembles a plate
is oval and empty.
No table, no food.
Everything lies
in the *mise en scène*, the ready-
made notion that looks
transcend substance—
a crotchet
and a conviction. Rotate
the image ninety
degrees to the right.

The fork—
flayed in midsentence,
into two shadows.
Modeled on its
reflection, it tilts
from invention.
Alignment becomes
gray and shy.
Roundness in vain, the plate
must plot
an empty chalice. Rotate
the image ninety
degrees one more time.

Under siege, the fork
and the plate play

bait and switch,
victims of an eclipse,
shifting concept of light.
In a picture, this matters: umbra
and penumbra, which is
more pertinent.
Rotate it back. Now,
tell me. When did you last
eat with your hands,
ruin a master-
piece out of folly?

OM DHRUNG SVAHA

Chase the wind on your tongue
Shadows, let's rally a storm
Scoop out stars from a lake
at the fate of hills that mourn
The phoenix chews a cage
Caterpillars tour in sad shoes
Ask. Every strand of hair
Pull the trigger. Stop the rocking
After hierarchy, a mule, straw planes
Walk as if you've Greek blood
If I speak for the dead, I must
Eat the sun. If I speak for them
Fingernails to the dirt, my hands
Comb the grass. A cricket, alone
It spits out a tongue. Every flight
imitates smoke and a corpse
Gulp it down. Buffoons, tsars, monks,

silenced by daggers and ochre walls
in a slave kitchen, a birth kept secret
or cajole tombs, hyenas on the loose
their glee. A hidden gear is moving oceans
dust is feasted with bronze embers
jiving their bodies into the free zone
wires the password of afterlife
horse, it floats like an orphan
beasts in praise of sleep and lunacy
running in the veins. Belief / disbelief
tap this orangutan out of my mind
I write on water and live blind
press the wind between their palms
in this field. I want the moon to strip
of gulls gone, gone without a trace
I am motherless. Like this bowl of earth
and presidents. It's time to say *gloria*—

MY HIROSHIGE

Rain. Splatters. In parallel black lines. Straight. Tilted right. From a blacker cloud. On a bridge. Which has no arch. Huddled, miniature, and discreet. Men under oil-paper umbrellas. Or a straw hat, or a blanket. In short kimonos. Rushing. Brushing off one another. In opposite directions. A boat struggled upstream. Long and lonely. On a cork coaster. Print from the Victoria and Albert Museum. Perfect dimensions. A shot of tequila served with olives. In a train. Fields. Wind. Fast and past. Heading for a rural village north of Kagawa.

PEINTRE

Where the bamboo clacked
in broad light, you

thought the image

out of sight. Metronome
ticked, wondering

about time. Fingers
slow, you closed

both eyes to train a cathedral

of silence without lies. Something
fluttered, you couldn't

see why. Too bare, too alike.
Was it a stupa

of colors, down

to the thread? A bell rang
twice, you realized

it was there,

slanting by your side,

the voice of summer rain, the last
Manchurian sky.

JARDINS SOUS LA PLUIE

All things considered, details render rain
free of glory, even more feral
than disfigured fountains
hoping to be illicit yet failing
in their drive.

       Pleasure is different
when flesh answers to water—
the act of receiving, a cold triumph.
The way rain sends gladness
from sky to my fingers.

       How do poets speak
ill of flowers, make apparent
their break of lightness? Facts be
shown in what's wild and bare,
glamour replaces the first half of nature.

       Like the old masters,
I seek a shape for rain. A form, a word,
something hard to fake. How foolish
I am to whitewash thoughts
into suitcases of cloud

       only to find—*May you feel*
them rise—Monet and Debussy kept
rain with discomfort, trying to measure
a quiet too pure
and transparent for humans.

Notes

The epigraph by János Pilinszky is from "Complaint" (1948), translated from the Hungarian by János Csokits and Ted Hughes, in *The Desert of Love: Selected Poems* (Anvil Press Poetry, 1989).

"I Wait for the Ruined Elegance"

The first line is after the last verse of my translation "Mirror," by contemporary Chinese poet Zhang Zao, forthcoming from Zephyr Press.

"In the Thick of It"

The quotation is translated from the Chinese by Eva Hung in Gu Cheng's *Selected Poems* (Renditions Paperbacks, 1990).

From Tomaž Šalamun, *Turning the head is a total utopia* and *The space reserved for a terrible long sleep,* translated from the Slovenian by the author with Phillis Levin and Thomas Kane, respectively.

Stanza eight alludes to a poem of Gu Cheng, translated as "Smokestacks" by Joseph R. Allen in *Sea of Dreams: The Selected Writings of Gu Cheng* (New Directions, 2005). Gu wrote the poem at age twelve.

"Partita, but Nothing to Do with Bach"

Karol Szymanowski (1882–1937) was a Polish composer and pianist. His best-known piano compositions include *Métopes* (1915)—a cycle of three tone poems ("The Sirens' Isle," "Calypso," and "Nausicaa") based on Greek mythology—and *Masques* (1916).

"An Uprising Committed to Longhand"

The quotation is translated from the French by A. J. Krailsheimer in Blaise Pascal's *Pensées* (Penguin Classics, 1995).

"Geneviève de Gaulle-Anthonioz took more than fifty years before writing Ravensbrück down in *La Traversée de la nuit*"

A member of the French Resistance, Geneviève de Gaulle-Anthonioz (1920–2002) was arrested by the Gestapo in 1943. Deported to Ravensbrück, she was a hostage deemed valuable by the Germans during negotiations and was kept alive in isolation until the war ended. In 1998 she broke her silence in a memoir of less than fifty pages (translated by Richard Seaver as *The Dawn of Hope*). *My eyes,* she wrote, *close into a kind of interior vision: a big, peaceful lake in the middle of a dark forest. The shores of the lake are steep and bare. Not a reed, not a ripple, not a bird.*

Acknowledgments

Several poems, often in earlier form, first found a home in *ABZ, American Literary Review, Antigonish Review, Barrow Street, Bitter Oleander, Mānoa, Paris/Atlantic, Salamander, Spoon River Poetry Review, Vallum,* and *Witness.*

I am deeply grateful to Jeffrey Greene, Barbara Yien, Sally Molini, Bai Hua, Mark Strand, Lee Sharkey, and Susan Thomas.

Princeton Series of Contemporary Poets